Saving Our Singles

101

Ways The Church Can Reach The Single Parent

By Mary Beth Riggins

Published by Westview, Inc., Nashville, Tennessee

Copyright © 2008 Mary Beth Riggins.

All Rights Reserved. No portion of this book may be reproduced in any fashion, either mechanically or electronically, without the express written permission of the author. Short excerpts may be used with the permission of the author or the publisher for the purposes of media reviews.

First Edition, May 2008

Printed in the United States of America on acid-free paper.

ISBN 978-0-9816172-5-1

Prepress by Westview Book Publishing, Inc.

PUBLISHED BY WESTVIEW, INC.
P.O. Box 210183
Nashville, Tennessee 37221
www.publishedbywestview.com

To Cody

My Co-Author and Inspiration

You wrote this book by living it.

Single Parents Must Be:

Bankers

Nurses

Teachers

Counselors

Chauffeurs

Cooks

Comforters

Carpenters

Mechanics...

And then they go to work!

Author's Note

Statistics are showing that, unfortunately, divorce is constantly on the rise in the American Society. The Church, as a body of believers, can do much more to reinforce that all families need love and acceptance. If you find just one idea in this book that will help or encourage a single parent family, then I have achieved my goal.

Table of Contents

When Divorce Happens 1
In the Event of a Death...7
At School..15
Around The House 23
Cars and Maintenance 31
At Church 37
Financial...43
To Help With Single Parent Boys...51
Help With Daughters of Single Parent Dads.........................61
How To Help With Holidays 67
Miscellaneous Helps 73

"God has given each of you some special abilities: be sure to use them to help each other, passing on to others God's many kinds of blessings."
I Peter 4:10   (The Living Bible)

When Divorce Happens

The soon to be divorced parent may not know where to find the correct courtroom, or where to park downtown. Offer to pick them up and drive them to the courthouse.

Attend the final divorce hearing with the now single parent. Be there for moral support.

Take them to lunch afterwards, and begin to plan positively for the future.

Listen! Listen! Listen! Let them talk about their fears, concerns, and doubts. Listen in love, and reassure them that God isn't finished with them yet.

Suggest counseling for the children if needed, and help locate a Christian counselor.

In the Event of a Death

Make phone calls for them; notify other church members.

Arrange to pick up the children at school.

Offer to go with them to make funeral arrangements, and other difficult decisions.

Drive them to the visitation.

At the funeral home, write down the names of those bringing in food, or doing other acts of kindness.

Provide hand lotion, breath mints, and Kleenex to the family when greeting the guests at visitation.

Offer to stay at their home during the funeral service to receive food, flowers, or guests.

Wash their car, and see that it is filled with gas for the drive to the burial.

Be sure the children have clean and appropriate clothing for the funeral. Offer to help bathe and dress the little ones.

If the funeral is out of town, offer your frequent flyer miles so they may attend.

Offer to feed and water pets if they go out of town for a funeral.

At School

School supplies are expensive. Pick up an extra box of crayons, pencils or pack of notebook paper when you go to the store.

When snow days keep the children home for the day, offer to keep the children so the parent can go on to work. It is vital that single parents get to work!

Save Boxtops For Education, Campbell's Soup labels or whatever their school is collecting.

Be on the approved list for picking up the children from school. Students will never be released to your care without this prior arrangement. This is especially important in the case of inclement weather or an early dismissal.

Know the route and times of the car pool, or bus number in case of an emergency.

Pass along or purchase school uniforms or dress code appropriate clothing.

During the parent-teacher conference, be available to keep the remaining siblings at home. It is difficult to concentrate on what the teacher is saying when you are trying to watch for the other Kids.

Show your support by attending ballgames, graduations, and recitals.

Offer to bake cupcakes for a class party.

Buy whatever the kids are selling for their school, scouts, or ball team.

Offer to take older kids to college weekends at colleges they may be interested in attending.

Around The House

28.

Offer to put together swing sets, bicycles, and play houses.

29.

Let the single parent know that you will be available to wait for repairmen at their home. This eliminates the need of them taking off work.

30.

Winterize the lawn mower, and any other lawn care equipment.

31.

After a winter storm, help remove limbs and debris from the yard. Shovel snow if necessary.

32.

Share a rental carpet cleaner, or any item you would rent. Both of you can use it, and cut the expenses in half.

33.

If the children are small, offer to help cut and trim the yard. If there are older teens, teach them how to use a weed-eater.

34.

Plan a yard sale together, and share the work, the fun, and the profits.

35.

Encourage single parents to invest in a good security system. The peace of mind will outweigh the expense. A Sunday School class might want to help with this as a project.

36.

When upgrading your appliances, check to see if they are need of them. Your old appliances may be newer than what they are now using.

37.

Give the kids an opportunity to earn money.

Cars and Maintenance

38.

Encourage them to have emergency roadside service. (AAA is a good example.) Always carry a cell phone with you.

39.

Teach the single Mom how to use jumper cables.

40.

Check her tires for uneven wear and the need for rotation.

41.

When buying a vehicle, offer to go with them if you know a lot about cars. Women often don't know what questions to ask.

42.

Check the vehicle for anti-freeze. Teach her to "winterize" her vehicle, and what emergency items to carry in her trunk.

43.

Have the men in the church hold an "oil change" Saturday for single Moms.

44.

Car tags are an expensive item. Check the license plate and see when the tags expire. It would be a great help if someone would assume this responsibility.

At Church

45.

Be sure that childcare is offered at every service.

46.

Refer to the single parent as the Smith family, and not Mary and Little Johnny. The children need the reinforcement that they are still very much a family.

47.

Subscribe to denominational literature for the single parents. It keeps them informed to missions work, and what is going on in other churches.

48.

If at all possible, don't put the single Mom on nursery roster. She needs the interaction with other Christian adults.

49.

Pay all or part of summer church camp for the single parent family. This provides life long Bible training for children and allows the parent some much needed down time.

50.

If your church offers Christian financial classes, help pay for them and their older teen to attend. Financial Peace University and Crown Financial Ministries are excellent sources of solid Biblical financial training.

51.

Invite them over for Sunday dinner.

52.

Take the children with you to places of service. The Red Cross, summer mission trips and Ronald McDonald house are reminders that others have needs that they can help to meet.

Financial

53.

If you have an attorney in your church, have them meet with the single parents to insure they have a written will. Even if they feel they have no estate, they must outline their wishes for distribution of the children in case of an emergency.

54.

Discuss the need for having a "Trusted family friend." This person needs to have access to medical information, names and phone numbers of all family members. They must have signed permission to act on behalf of the parent in case of an emergency. Someone other than the parent MUST have written permission to admit a child for medical care.

55.

If you have an insurance agent in the church, meet with them to discuss auto, homeowners, and health coverage. This is not the time to make a sale, rather a time to minister to them thru your knowledge and experience.

56.

Encourage the single parent to open a savings account for each child. The amount of savings is not important, it is the habit of saving that will serve as an example for your children.

57.

Pay a winter utility bill anonymously.

58.

Help with a do-able budget. Encourage her to tithe, as God is faithful in keeping His promises to provide for us. A good rule of thumb is 10% tithe, 10% savings, and the remainder for living expenses. Encourage them to stay away from debt!

59.

Share the cost of a Sam's or Costco card. Plan, shop, and divide, and both of you will save money on paper goods and groceries.

60.

Vacations are not usually in the budget for single parent families. Share your time share or beach cottage if you are unable to use it, and want to provide them with an inexpensive vacation.

61.

Pass along winter coats, baby clothes and sports equipment. These are used for such a short time, and can ease the strained budget of single parents.

62.

Swap and share coupons, magazines, and kids' DVDs.

To Help with Single Parent Boys

63.

Build a trusting relationship with the boy. This works best with a happily married man with a desire to make a difference in the boy's life.

64.

Invite him over for football games or sports events on television. This makes for great male bonding.

65.

Take them thru Hunter's Safety class (with parental permission). Take them hunting on opening day of the Season.

66.

Teach them how to responsibly use and clean a gun.

67.

Take them fishing. Barter with them to pay for their license.

68.

Help them start a tackle box and how to take care of it.

69.

Teach them how them how to clean the fish they caught! Have a camera ready for a picture of this special moment to frame and give to Mom.

70.

Show them the correct way to wash a car.

71.

Pass along scouting and camping equipment. Take them on over night camp outs with friends.

72.

Teach them how to drive. There are some things that are not easy for a Mom to do!

73.

Show them how to tie a tie.

74.

If you are handy with basic tools, spend time showing them how to use them. Help start a tool box, and let them help with projects around the house. This will prove to be a great help to them in later years.

75.

Teach them the fundamentals of water safety and swimming.

Help with Daughters of Single Parent Dads

Use any of the ideas in the previous chapter if your single-parented girls have similar interests.

76.

Encourage your daughter to form a close bond with a happily married woman in your Church. Ask if she is willing to answer many questions- always from the standpoint of a woman committed to Christ. Be sure this is regarded as a serious and time consuming responsibility.

77.

Be available to hold sleepovers at your home. Many parents will not allow their girls to spend the night when a Mom is not in the home.

78.

Plan shopping trips for new school clothes and to get new haircuts.

79.

Teach the girls basic cooking skills and routine kitchen management.

80.

Take her to buy her first bra, and female hygiene supplies.

How to Help with Holidays

81.

Help the child bake a birthday cake for the single parent.

82.

Make a videotape of the special events in their lives. Be there to take pictures of graduations, birthdays and holidays.

83.

Include single parent families in your Holiday dinners and celebrations. This gives the children a secure feeling of extended family.

84.

Take their picture for the Christmas card. Again, this reinforces to others they are very much a family unit.

85.

Take the children Christmas caroling. This gives the single parent time to wrap presents, and fill stockings without prying eyes.

86.

Make Mother's Day and Father's Day special for single parents. Many times they receive no recognition on this day. By helping the children realize the importance, you are teaching them to honor their future husband/ wife in later years.

87.

October 31st is not a good time to leave a home unattended. Offer to stay at the single parent's home so they may attend a Fall Fest or church activity.

Miscellaneous Helps

88.

Offer to keep the children so the single parent can go and vote. This could be a great learning lesson for an older child to go with the parent and observe the importance of good citizenship.

89.

Take pictures often of the single parent families. Many have few pictures of themselves and the children together. The Mom or Dad is always the one taking the picture.

90.

At the grocery store when they have a "BOGO" (buy one get one), share the "get one" with a single parent family. You'll both get the benefit.

91.

Take the younger children to the Library for story time. This frees up the parents for an hour, and is fun and educational for the children.

92.

When a single parent has a child in the hospital, offer to keep the other children at their home, and help maintain their regular schedule.

93.

Encourage single parents to take care of themselves physically. Remind them to have regular dental checkups, mammograms, and physicals.

94.

Children form very tight attachments to pets when going thru the loss of a parent. Single parents often cannot afford the additional budget strain of pet food, and Rover is forced to leave the home. To keep this from happening, buy a bag of pet food and put where they can find it. This is actually a need, rather than a want.

95.

Spring is Rabies shot time. Ask the children of single parents to take your pet to the clinic. Pay them for taking your pet along and getting his shot, too.

96.

When cooking a large meal of spaghetti or a favorite casserole, make a double portion. Share with the single parent family for a welcome treat. It takes very little effort as you are already cooking.

97.

Encourage single parents to continue their education. Whether it's a GED or an M.Ed, they will set a good example for their children to finish what they start.

98.

Attend a Father-Daughter or Mother-Son function with them at school.

99.

In the Spring, help them plant a garden. This is a good family activity and also provides help with the food budget.

100.

Ball teams can be an expensive item for any family. Offer to provide the Cokes and refreshments when it is time for the single parent to provide them.

101.

Most importantly, love them, pray for them and encourage them. Jesus said whatever we do for others, we are essentially doing it for Him.

I would enjoy hearing ways your church is helping the single parent family in your church or community.
Please contact me at
MaryBeth@parentingbyone.com or
P.O.Box 155, Watertown, TN 37184